ISTHMUS

ISTHMUS

Poems

by

Dan Rifenburgh

Mutabilis Press
Houston

Copyright © 2013 by Daniel Rifenburgh
Foreword Copyright © 2013 by Paul Christensen
All rights reserved

ISBN 978-0-9729432-7-7
Library of Congress Control Number: 2013943757

Cover photo by Paola Rifenburgh

Published by

Mutabilis Press
Houston, TX

www.mutabilispress.org

In Memoriam

Donald Justice

1925 — 2004

Come back now and help me with these verses.
Whisper to me some beautiful secret that you remember from life.

Donald Justice, *Invitation To A Ghost*

FOREWORD

Isthmus is a good book of poems, by which I mean the author is in control of what he wants to do, writes clearly, and pursues his main theme without digressing. The theme is the "isthmus" of his title, which he defines and locates as the narrow bridge connecting vast polar realities, referred to as the light and the dark of human experience. He's not the first to try to connect these opposites of body and the soul, good and evil, virtue and corruption. Dante majestically links up hell, purgatory and heaven in *The Divine Comedy*; Milton gathered up most of what we know about joy and grief in his companion poems, *L'Allegro* and *Il Penseroso*; Blake's *The Marriage of Heaven and Hell* upends our usual definitions of those two fates by making hell seem energetic and interesting, and heaven a bit tedious as the place where "eager beavers" get their just rewards.

Rifenburgh, now a flatbed truck driver after a desultory career as a college adjunct teacher, steps into this tradition with gusto and realism. He has a keen eye for detail, and a practicality about his vision that restrains a tendency toward the oracular, a trait I sometimes noted in his first book, *Advent* (2002). Now the middle-aged poet is less given to riffs and expansions, and keeps to the matter at hand, holding the extremes of emotion in some sort of balance. And why not? At 64 years of age, you are likely to know that every happiness has its shadow, and every sorrow its lesson. In "Life 101," he puts his education in dark experience plainly:

> Thus we received the usual poor letters
> In deportment, even as we put on
> The knowledge we'd come for
>
> And were issued, with the pomp
> Of a dark, swelling music, our silky
> Black gowns and tiltable mortars.

And the dark has its humorous side, as he notes in "The Dead," where the departed reproach the living "and we don't know why," and "sail on the morning tide/ For Elysium,/ Tennis racquets in hand." Here is fresh language, and a powerful originality in giving us back experience we had not perceived this way before.

The poem "Isthmus" contains some of his most powerful language, and takes lyric to a sustained eloquence. The scene is Macchu Picchu, the "sky city" of the Incas, and represents at least one way to imagine the celestial light of heaven, but at the same time, the ruins of a city that had tried to grasp that dream of spiritual perfection. Rifenburgh is quick to note that here again is a kind of delicate isthmus between the lofty state of the gods and the merely human, a "Panama," as he tells his "East L.A. *chicano* " friend, Javier. The panorama he sees next is a whole congeries of inflected, tightly bound contradictory states, the snowy tops of Vulcan Irazu "In the middle of the Costa Rican isthmus,"

> So high, so cold at that elevation
> Yet hot lava boiling in the caldera beneath
> And in the distance the cool,
> Blue line of the Pacific Ocean
> And in the other direction the thin line of the Atlantic.

Which recalls the "wandering Arab of Al-Andaluz,"

> Ibn Al-Arabi, that Platonic soul
> Who said this life is a brief isthmus
> Between two seas, the sea of material things
> And the sea of intellectual things . . .

Such is the "bridge between two such continents,"

> The fiery and holy cauldron of the mind
> And the passionate guts below,
> Body and soul. . .

He shows himself a true poet in these lines, able to sustain a lofty and cerebral argument in common language, and never lose the thread of his idea in a sudden fit of lyric hyperbole.

Rifenburgh doesn't buy into the experimental tradition that raged all through the last century, and ended by shredding the poem into gibberish. The art of song was dead by the time the "L*a*n*g*u*a*g*e" poets were through with it. Nothing about language was to be trusted in that age of anti-establishment cynicism. But Rifenburgh had his own poets to believe in, among them Pablo Neruda, Cesar Vallejo, Rainer Maria Rilke, Adam Zagajewski, Heraclitus, Poe, his mentor Donald Justice, and even a sometimes doughty Anthony Hecht – who never lost faith in the power of lyric to make sense of human emotion. He has absorbed that faith and carries on, staying just shy of the abyss of disillusionment less wary poets approached and sometimes fell into.

In *Isthmus*, we have masterful renderings of the villanelle in "These Written Words, Like Paintings" and "For the Spoken Word"; two-line poems (among his favorite forms), tercets, quatrains, and a powerful elegy, "After Justice," where his major theme is recaptured elegantly in the lines

> Someone climbing up from under a bridge
> Will pull out a harmonica and, weakly at first,
> Begin to play.
>   He will find for us a tune
> Recalling all that we have suffered
> Through having existed, but altered,
> As music alters everything.
> . . .
>
> We'll see the universe then, in the light of God's mercy,
> As a field of diamonds: playful, winking diamonds.
> This sadness now we'll see as sweet then,
> And we'll smile.

—Paul Christensen

ACKNOWLEDGEMENTS

I wish to thank the School of Graduate Studies of the University of Texas at Austin and the Texas Institute of Letters for the benefit of a six-month Dobie Paisano Fellowship; thanks to the Sewanee Writers Conference for a Tennessee Williams Scholarship; to the West Chester Poetry Conference for a Frederick Morgan Scholarship; to Phillip Hoy of Waywiser Press, London, for organizing a UK reading tour: for individual invitations to read I thank the W.H. Auden Society of Christ Church College, Oxford; the Oxford University Poetry Society; the Royal Festival Hall, London; the Wordsworth Trust at Dove Cottage, Grasmere and the late Michael Donaghy for inviting me to meet with his workshop at City University, London; I wish also to thank the National Endowment For The Arts (NEA) for inviting me to serve as a participating writer, workshop instructor and editorial panelist on the *Operation Homecoming* national initiative and anthology.

Some of the poems previously appeared in these literary journals and anthologies: *Texas Review; Tampa Review; War, Literature and the Arts; Shenandoah; Southwest Review; Literature and Belief; Colorado Review; Lyric Review;* and from Houston's Mutabilis Press: *Time Slice: Houston Poetry 2005,* an anthology (2005); *The Weight Of Addition: An Anthology of Texas Poetry* (2007) and *Improbable Worlds: An Anthology of Texas and Louisiana Poets* (2012). A few of the poems appeared in unrevised form in *Advent,* Waywiser Press, London: 2002.

My deepest appreciation and gratitude goes to my wife, Paola, and to my son, William.

CONTENTS

Proem: For Angel Gonzalez	17
The Catastrophe	19
Sea Wind, Pompano	21
Bodies Flying Out Of Towers	22
Cesar Vallejo: *Los Heraldos Negros*	24
September Armor	25
Music For Dead Angels	27
Out Of The Creek Hollow	29
Codicil To Be Appended To The City Charter	30
Others: To Adam Zagajewski	31
Tycho Brahe's *Nova Stella*	33
Life 101	35
The Dead	36
My Wife At Daybreak Singing	37
Requital For Fire	38
Another World	40
Tolstoy: With Napoleon In Flight From Moscow, General Kutuzov Speaks To His Troops Near Dobroe, 1812	41
The Fragments Of Heraclitus	43
Cum Laude	44
These Written Words, Like Paintings	46
Wild Turkeys At Paisano	47
Anthony Hecht Departs: An Adieu	48
An Ice Cream Truck Goes By	49
Return	50

Racing Form	51
On Epstein's Statue "Jacob And The Angel" At The Tate Gallery	53
Mother	55
Pablo Neruda Comes Flying	56
At A Vatican Exhibition	58
The Unicorn	59
For The Spoken Word	60
Uncle Kenny	61
Isthmus	62
My Father's Will	64
Notes On A Meeting	66
On My Last Day	67
After Justice	68
The New Poems	75
Some Notes On The Poems	77
Biographical Note	79

ISTHMUS

PROEM: FOR ANGEL GONZALEZ

In our veins, so tough yet coy a double-
Helix, pointing in the dark there.

I can see it: now determined, now ambivalent:
A small boat, tightly-caulked,

Double-prowed,
Swiftly agile,

A finger toward the future and the past,
Wanting to go two ways at once, x-rayed

In the flash of a dark thought. Odd, that
The dark itself never enjoys the drama of setting,

Just gets chased away by the sun, so fast,
Rudely scattered, though it's always lurking

Someway in the corners, flees into
Old boxes, fountain pens,

The veins of poets. In the small package
Of a poem one hears sometimes the music

Of two darknesses meeting, two cities
Exchanging freight trains,

Conversing until dawn.
Keep the poem dirty, you said, Angel,

Dirty with the smoky night of veins.
Pour the darkness of a throat into

The darkness of a poem
And watch the small boat, then,

This shell-swirled
Codex,

Visible in a flash, rock and lift
On swells of the pulse,

Trembling with mortality, rushing
Like the poem to its destiny:

"Poet," spoke
An Angel,

"Spit the darkness of a mouth
Into the dark poem."

THE CATASTROPHE

> *Dog to coyote to wolf,*
> *The cry went forth,*
> *Able to Baker to you.*
>   — Henri Coulette

It was dormant awhile, latent
In several pockets, fingered lightly,

Then it was at throats, brandished in the air,
Then slicing through clouds over water,
A drawer of knives falling out of the sun.

Now it is a bloom of fiery tulips,
A shattering of crystal,
And now a hooded viper rising in the air.

It flies off transmitters,
Flickers on tv screens, retinas
And unrolls itself from cylindrical presses.

It is quartered, chopped, bundled
And dumped from the backs
Of slowly rolling trucks.
And it grows. It sits down
To lunch with multitudes, passing the salt.

It tangles itself with music, filters down
With the sawings of ardent violins.
The yellow light of the radio dial is sweating with it.
The conductor furiously mops his brow.

And now it is a wraith of a crack whore,
Spindly and woven of silt and soot,
Advancing gamely on stiletto heels,
Stepping to a jagged tango and thrusting forth
The hollow of her open hand.

My feet are gliding towards her.
My heavy arms rise to open.

She is whispering in my ear now
And taking firmly my hand:
Look,
We are dancing.

After Justice

SEA WIND, POMPANO

You seem to rise tonight
From the lapping, black waves below,
No less dark, nor less troubled, than they

Yet all you are is space, movement,
A restlessness that blows and blows.
What to make of you?

Before one can answer,
You have subsided, seemingly nameless,
And, subsiding, die;

Yet, in the leaning stance
Of a sea grape tree, westward
Casting its boughs,

The tilted scrawl
Of your signature:
Sea wind, Pompano.

After Rilke, Justice

BODIES FLYING OUT OF TOWERS

> *... history, that never sleeps or dies*
> *And, held one moment, burns the hand.*
> — Auden

They are descending toward the street,
A street we knew.

Had we met them there before,
Freshly discharged from the elevators,

We might have talked, might have entered
A bar together and had a drink.

Our talk would not have been exceptional,
But normal. Not like this.

Perhaps we even envied them.
That was how things were then.

After a time
We would have strolled back out again,

Observing the cool, chuted air
Above the street, such lofty shafts

As provide a concourse
For weary spirits, coming late out of a bar's enclosure,

That spirits might, ascending skyward,
Go trafficking briefly with the afternoon light

Like the cotes of pigeons from Battery Park
Mounting on the updrafts there,

Or like that cunning courier, Hermes,
Wing-footed, lithe,

And able to pace weightlessly, at will, the empty air:
That quicksilver one commissioned

To swiftly retrieve and bear
Heavenward all earnest, earth-spoken prayer.

CESAR VALLEJO: *LOS HERALDOS NEGROS*

There are blows in life, so strong…I don't know!
Blows like the wrath of God, as if before them
The distillation of all suffering
Pools in the soul…I don't know!

They are few, but they exist…opening dark trenches
In the fiercest face and in the strongest back.
They are perhaps the horses of barbarous Attilas
Or the black heralds Death sends to us.

They are the plummetings of Christs of the soul,
Of some once-adored faith that Destiny blasphemes.
These sanguinary blows seem the crackling
Of some bread by the oven's door, burning us.

And the man, poor man…*pobre!* He turns his eyes
As when, over the shoulder, a loud hand-clap calls us:
Turns his crazed eyes, and all that he has lived
Pools in his gaze like a pool of guilt.

There are blows in life, so strong…I don't know!

SEPTEMBER ARMOR

Tinted visors click shut
On helmeted heads: objects

On the periphery matter, but now
Cannot be so easily seen.

Only the glaring, obvious things are observed,
Not the backlit fringes of clouds,

No lamplight in towers
Pouring into mirrors,

Candescing a woman's necklace
And face, not the text

In the iridescent
Mother-of-pearl

And only the shrieks of gulls,
Buffeted by the winds,

Reach the shell of the ear
From the Upper Harbor.

Dusk considers dusty billows
Suspended over the wounded city

And the fire, lapping at the tongue's root,
Smolders, flees through arterial conduits,

Passing subterranean trains, distancing, in dreams,
Gray hulls with their gray guns gliding

Above polyparies of coral,
And reaches into arms, hands, with the smoky oil

Of its rigor. Every head is covered,
Each foot shod.

Mud cannot find
Toes. Earth

Cannot find her husband.
Now the sleepy wards of old locks

Remember suddenly the bite
Of arsenal keys turning in them,

Shunting brass tumblers aside,
Opening the great doors of September.

MUSIC FOR DEAD ANGELS: VARIATIONS ON A TEXT BY ALBERTI

they fall out of eternity from a sadness
that collects like sludge in the memory
seizing the flared pinions of their wings

search for them
in the insomnia of waste pipes

ditches clotted by idle trash
a trampled star
lost things

for I have smelled them swathed in the sour mists
settling on heaps of refuse

they stare tenaciously
from the empty sockets of eyelets
stamped in the sides of worn-out shoes

in all this
the vacant places
cinder
susurrus

for I have touched them
in the lesser desert of a broken brick
come to nothing from tenement
and wheelbarrow

I have seen them
in those near-human absences rickety,
discarded chairs support

the dead angels
almost weightless

quietly sitting

as if we had some part
in the way they now cannot leave us

OUT OF THE CREEK HOLLOW

Percussive wings slap,
Startle the air,
Lifting the feathered craft
Of a great blue heron,
Oaring him now
Farther down the hollow.

CODICIL TO BE APPENDED TO THE CITY CHARTER

I remember liberating with difficulty her white
Breasts from the white brassiere. We were coming of age

In the leafy woods of young mammals.
Later, we moved to the city

And were given jobs and instruction. Industry hummed.
You could buy a color tv, drapes. There was nothing

That could not be insured against loss.
Some people spent whole days in offices

Writing up the policies, charmed by the reasonableness
The ages had granted human affairs.

These were among those most taken aback
When that noble lady, the mother of the king,

Held by its mane what she thought was
The severed head of a lion, but when she looked closer

It was the head of her son. He had given offense
To a vine-wreathed god, and the god had put

A special madness on her. With bloody hands
She quit the plaza and sped into exile,

Wailing beyond the walls of the city
But where had been woods was now wasteland

And in that desert she fed only on heartbreak
And soft, plaintive cries of the panthers.

OTHERS: TO ADAM ZAGAJEWSKI

> *The others are not Hell*
> *If you see them early, their*
> *Foreheads pure, cleansed by dreams.*
> — *Adam Zagajewski*

In another's poem
I went to Lvov

(i.e., a city in eastern Poland,
Or, the Polish Ukraine,

Sometimes Russia, Germany,
Austria, too; Napoleon,

Short of stature
But long on ambition,

Was once heard here on a prominence
Speaking Corsican French

With the ghost
Of Genghis Khan.)

Now I find
I can't get out of Lvov.

I've become that eccentric uncle, the one
With drooping, gray mustaches and bulbous nose

Writing off in a corner a long poem called *"Why,"*
Dedicated to The Almighty.

Adam, come to Lvov,
To a place on that street

Halfway between your birth-house
And the birth-house of Mr. Cogito

And, under a linden tree,
Kick up the dust there.

I'm actually still here in Texas
But even Texas, now, has become Lvov.

Texan dust has become
Lvov dust.

That's what the discourse of others
Might do for one.

Near where the brisket smokes on the barbeque,
On a little wooden cutting board,

Sit our expired exit visas, once
Our means of escape from Lvov,

And a draft there, wind-fluttered pages
Of the ninth, final canto,

The justifying coda
To an encyclopedic poem entitled, *"Why."*

Adam, come to Lvov,
We have strawberries, white napkins

And, now, brisket, poems, all
Dedicated to The Almighty, and others,

To their ennobling discourses,
Their sober dialogues,

The means by which
We all arrived here, in springtime, at Lvov.

TYCHO BRAHE'S *NOVA STELLA*

Soon after Michelangelo died a brilliant star
That was not there the night before, now was.

It was the eleventh night of the eleventh month,
A time already freighted with penultimacy

And dark forebodings of last things: now,
This calling card, perhaps, of a chill or hot

Apocalypse, portentous and frightening,
Hanging in the air. It was set within a rectangle

Of four known stars of Cassiopeia
And shone brighter than bright Venus,

At first whitely, then became yellow,
Then gradually a martial, sanguinary red

And, diminishing, took on
The hue and bluff caste of lead.

For sixteen months it hung there,
Instilling wonder and terror, then, mysteriously,

Was gone. Many years later,
The poet Edgar Allan Poe wrote

The star had come to pick up the soul of the artist
And poet, Michelangelo Buonarroti.

It arrived like a celestial taxi,
But was also Michelangelo's new home,

Some luminous, exclusive yacht that, moored
A little ways out from shore,

Soon enough received
Its honored passenger, weighed anchor,

Departed, and has been seen no more.
This from a poet, ill-starred, who ended

Bedeviled in a gutter in Baltimore.

LIFE 101

In the second term of our matriculation
A small joke waved through the classroom
And we couldn't figure out how to stop it.

When the teacher threatened us with failure
We paused momentarily, then
Laughed even louder,

For the shadow
Of death was passing through us:
Dark water through frail filters.

The grail of our laughter
Poured outside the classroom windows,
Slaked the iron thirst of the grates of sewers,

Swam on its own stream
To the chalkboard
And there bisected a perfect circle.

Like a radiant knife, haloed with dust motes,
It caressed a moment, for the sake
Of a secret geometry, the heart of the *here*

Which prefigures *here*after
And left such longings and languor in us
As befuddle, at times, brave philosophers.

Thus we received the usual poor letters
In deportment, even as we put on
The knowledge we'd come for

And were issued, with the pomp
Of a dark, swelling music, our silky
Black gowns and tiltable mortars.

THE DEAD

The dead don't care for us.
They grimace as we file past,
Regretting they were once tender toward us.

They won't assist us with probating their wills,
Much less carrying their heavy coffins.

Their wax faces are a reproach,
As if we are doing something (what,
We don't know) quite wrong.

The dead sail on the morning tide
For Elysium,
Tennis racquets in hand,

Accusing us from the deck rails,
Leaving worm-holes trailing through
The pulp of our days, vacancies

We cannot fill with wine,
Nor with remorse,

And, from this shore,
One cannot even get at them
To slap them for their insolence.

No, it's like this:
The dead repose long leagues from us,
Among golden isles and gentled hills,

Insufferably poised,
Marvelously self-contained,
And impossible to kill.

After Angel Gonzalez

MY WIFE AT DAYBREAK SINGING
IN SPANISH A PSALM OF ASCENTS

She will lift up
Her eyes, she sings,
To the mountains, to Jehova,

Where comes her succor,
Donde vendra mi socorro,
Though there are no mountains

In coastal east Texas
And the battle god
Of that wandering tribe

Has not been noticed stopping
Here of late;
Yet she,

A source, a strength
Asks of *"Ae-o-VA"*
This succor

And lifts up her eyes,
As if to mountains,
Spreading her arms

Wide to receive
As she sings
And receives

And the faltering
Day comes on, as
If beckoned by one.

REQUITAL FOR FIRE

> *Now a new generation is sent down from high heaven*
> —Vergil

Silence that was golden
Is broken into miscellaneous

Coins, sounding
Where they're strung on taut

Strands of voice,
Agreeable in their variance:

All told: a few relics of old crimes
Mixed with laughing acanthus.

Behind this is mind, playing
As with a golden abacus, toting

Pythagorean numbers. This
Particular sum: wings of the Archangel

Michael; and this: his flaming sword,
Bright brand thrust into a rain

Of ashes called History.
Here a street becomes known by

The howls of the wild dogs
Who seem always to gather there

On the morning after a war is declared.
The man walking hurriedly down it, testing

The long muscles of his legs,
They know as a soldier today

And, tomorrow, a tax collector
Or priest. Man has no set purpose,

But the divine has. Therefore,
The hounds bear no animus for him, but grin

Behind lolling tongues, unabashed,
Though he disturb with dissonant tread

The debris of citadels that settled like ash
Once on the crowns of Ninevah.

ANOTHER WORLD

In the daybreak tracery of a willow,
In the musk of blanched grasses at noon,
In the ant carrying a fragment of a leaf somewhere, racing
Against sundown:

You are looking at something in this world
But as you peer more closely, you realize
You are no longer here, you are in that other world,
Where the mirrors empty,

Your son is an orphan, your parents
Passed on childless, unwed
And your lover
Grabs only armfuls of scented air.

Strange, then, returning
To this plangent, cuneiform world,
To hear your name on her lips, her breath
Shading into a casual sigh,

And to recall, haltingly,
To assemble (so to resemble)
What she means thereby.

Perhaps, you hope, it is that man who falls,
Dives and returns, descends to ascend again
(And she can follow) back
Into dew-wet, light-laced, delicate
Traceries of the willow.

For Paola Baca

TOLSTOY: WITH NAPOLEON IN FLIGHT FROM MOSCOW, GENERAL KUTUZOV SPEAKS TO HIS TROOPS NEAR DOBROE, 1812

"Here's the thing, brothers.
I know it's hard for you,
But what's to be done.
Be patient, it won't last long.
We'll see our guests off,
Then we'll have a rest,
The tsar will not forget your service.

"It's hard for you,
But still you're at home;
But they—see what they've come to.
Worse than the lowest beggars.

"While they were strong
We took no pity on ourselves
But now we can pity them.
They're also people. Right, lads?"

The men in the ranks looked at him
Sympathetically, with intent,
Respectfully puzzled eyes.
The old general paused. He felt
Their eyes on him, their puzzlement.

This was no way to leave them,
Not after all this. Slowly a smile, starlike,
Wrinkled the corners of his mouth.
He hung his head then, as if
In perplexity, and spoke again.

"But, that said,
Who invited them here?
It's their own doing.
Fuck them in the fucking ass!"

The men started laughing then,
Breaking ranks, guffawing,
And roared, "Hurrah!" and, again, "Hurrah!"
As the old general, for the first time
In the whole campaign, swung his whip
Across the backside of his mount
And rode off at a gallop.

THE FRAGMENTS OF HERACLITUS

> *The name of the bow is life, but its work is death.*
> The Fragments

The fragments of Heraclitus,
Compact, trenchant, inscrutable,

Are lovely in their resistance
To analysis. Therefore, from sympathy,

And, being immortal,
They sometimes assume human forms

To attend unnoticed the burials of critics.
They hold by their brims dark fedoras and,

Standing aloof, stolid, anonymous,
Listen respectfully to brief eulogies

While the great world sifts noiselessly
Down through time's latticework

And the bow named life,
Accomplishing its work, later

Sends them strolling like slow arrows
Away from these shaded gravesites,

Pacing back cleansed
Into birdsong and light.

CUM LAUDE

I am enrolled in the highly-trained
Tribe of the mandarin.
What of the gatherers of wood,
Bringers of water,
The darners of socks and mittens?
What of those others
For whom the codes are hidden?

Years of carrels, books,
Furious studying, (oft
Outwatching the Bear),
Deciphering old texts laid on skins
In black chararct'ry,
And I am enrolled in the highly-trained
Tribe of the mandarin.

As a stray allusion strewn
To enrich meaning or stay confusion
May but confound the neophyte
Or the occasional reader, then,
What of those others
For whom the codes are hidden:

The callow laborer, the indolent
Shopgirl, their desultory kin?
I have cut their simple hearts
Like an onion – no tears!
--And I am enrolled in the highly-trained
Tribe of the mandarin.

Having scaled the walls of a lush garden,
Alone and unbidden,
Where glass-bead gamers
Circle in on the final glamours,
I am quietly schooled by their scribes
In the folded mysteries of the mandarin.
What of those others,
For whom the codes are hidden?

after a journal entry by Milosz

THESE WRITTEN WORDS, LIKE PAINTINGS

Seem to talk to you as though they were clever,
But if you ask them anything about what they are saying
They go on telling you the same thing forever.

So Plato has Socrates, in the *Phaedrus*, declare
And his complaint, his words, so incisive, disarming,
Seem also to talk to you as though they were clever

But neither do they avail of questioning. Rather,
Frozen on the pages these ages unending,
They go on dumbly recounting the same thing forever:

That they are counters for wit, counterfeit intelligencers,
Clear or crimson jewels that, their facets shimmering,
Seem to wink at you as though they were smart; however,

Just once press them, why the strict typographer
Won't let them relax, respond, refine their meaning,
And they go on blithely recounting the same thing over.

Just so, dear reader, are these lines, scribbled by a writer
Who's soon absconded, even as they go on telling,
Like a busted watch or scene from Goya,
A fixed, unrelenting thing forever.

WILD TURKEYS AT PAISANO

From their roosts
Among the cedars
Wild turkeys come
Down to the morning meadow,
Stepping lightly through gray mist
Like living brushstrokes
Upon a silk panel.

I count five
And they are larger
Than one imagined,
Yet can fly
For brief spans,
And will,
When, of a sudden, they spy
An interloping human.

There they rise now, seeing me,
And go wheeling
Like the turning measures of a verse
Over the next line of oak and cedar
To settle in a meadow unseen
On the cool reverse of earth's
Upright, Chinese screen.

ANTHONY HECHT DEPARTS: AN ADIEU

Ave, unlikely infantryman, footsore avatar
Of truths of Pentateuch and Torah,
Conscience of a consciousness
That came abrupt upon
The death camps and the horror;
May hosannas follow
Who sings an imperium of light now
From the entropic shadows,
Intrepid and honorable
As some dear cousin
We knew once of Mary.

AN ICE CREAM TRUCK GOES BY

An ice cream truck goes by playing, monotonously,
"Pop Goes The Weasel," which sets my hounds
To howling. They do not howl at the moon,
For there is none, the sky being overcast this afternoon.
The sun is slowly declining in the west
And here, in this fading light, I read a sonnet
Of Donald Justice, entitled, "The Wall"
About the eviction of Adam and Eve
From Eden, that first garden.
The angels were entirely
Companionable then, and even God,
Working so hard on his early poems,
Could be seen strolling through
The morning mists, composing. Of course,
It was bound to end badly. The poem is like a postcard
Dropped into a mailbox somewhere east of Eden,
Somewhere obnoxious ice cream trucks roll through,
Declaring a weasel to hounds. Now the text of the poem
Becomes more difficult to see. Something, in this failing light,
About a Cherub, a sword, the darkness of the world
And a gate, closing now, forever,
And giant wings unfurled.

RETURN

I have come home tonight, tired
From a thousand-mile journey.

Mute pens lie
Like toppled pawns
On the darkened desk, wanting
To be picked up.

Little soldiers,
See the white queen, Beauty,
Swirling her skirts in the distance?

Tomorrow at dawn we'll rise
And start for her again

But now, let us lie down
In the mending dark yet awhile,
Liege-like
Beside our pitch-black
And dozing king,

His serene majesty,
Snoring Oblivion.

RACING FORM

In Shelley's last, unfinished poem,
in Shelley's great poem which is without closure
Because the poor poet drowned in water,
in Shelley's great "The Triumph of Life,"
The last word of which is "of "
And the whole thing stops right there
While Shelley goes out to take in a boat ride
(Talk about your Lethe and Nepenthe!),
We meet, according to Harold Bloom
And Lionel Trilling, "Rousseau,
Prophet of nature, serving
As a surrogate for Wordsworth, entering
The poem as Vergil, the guide to Shelley's Dante,"
And all of this is related to you by Rifenburgh.

It's much easier, and sometimes as rewarding,
To study the bloodlines of flat-track thoroughbreds,
Such as: *Raise A Bid* got out of *Botcha
Botcha's Bid*, or, *This
Is Enough* from *On To Glory*
Gave *This Is Glory*, especially if he won,
But Life always wins. It's got
By *Spirit* out of *Some Kinda Shit*
And the odds are a zillion to one
(Or, is it one to a zillion, I forget)
That Life is going to win,
Going to suck you in, and *Something Spritely*
Is the racing name of that foal.

How can you resist her?
Who said you should?

Shelley did;
Laid his pen aside for an hour
And died, gasping water for air, air
And Life.

I sat in my car outside the track
And counted my losses.
Life lay down with death beside me

And they had the nerve
To fornicate in front of me.

I was thinking, not of those few
At Athens or Jerusalem,
But of how *Mar Best* gave
Mon Go Fast by *Mongo*

And mon do go fast
But the colt, he finish last
And my money was wasted
Fast as life, fast as that,

Fast as was the track
Where the fleet hooves
Tossed up the turf;
The little clods of this our earth,
The quick, high flinging and falling of

ON EPSTEIN'S STATUE "JACOB AND THE ANGEL" AT THE TATE GALLERY

Clearly, by dawn, the struggle is over,
The contest ends, and the angel has won.

What of the snaking caravan
Of cattle, folk, and possessions Jacob
Sent before him across the muddy river?

      How will he reach it, thus defeated,
With his thigh bone out of its hip socket
(The angel's last, gymnastic maneuver),

So that he now cannot even arise
To his former stature, but must be propped
By the brace of arms wrapping his torso?

(But his thoughts are not on his possessions;
Rather, he has demanded a blessing.)

He, prior to this moment seen
Carved in alabaster, the very
Embodiment of the word, *insistent*,

Clasping the stranger, this man or angel,
The one who calls himself. "Why do you ask
My name?" and not letting go of him till

At last, just now, the winged being bent
Over Jacob and gave up his blessing,
Saying, "Now you shall be called by all
Peoples, *Who Struggles With God.*"

Here, in the moment just after that moment
The collapse, the letting go,
But, with a new name, as if a new man
And the tall angel, that greater power,
Does not let go the newly blessed man,

But supports him while the great name invades
His thigh bone to the marrow, by the joint
Of the hip, as if thus to prepare him

For the centuries to come,
As if all the freight, all the barges, of all
Of the rivers of the world will end here in this

Frail figure, an *agon* of a man,
This struggling thing, this injured, insistent name
Clasping this god
And the god clasping him.

For Annie Freud

MOTHER

Two weeks after her death
I thought I felt her ghost
Enter a stand of rain-drizzled pines,
Not to return.

We don't know
If there's a heaven. Will the circle
Be unbroken?

What we can do is watch rain fall
And speak the word "mother"
To a far stand of pines.

If that's all we can do
It may be sufficient,
A beneficence,
Like the slow saying of *Selah*,

Then a quietus
And rain, the solving rain, somehow
Soothing as it falls, pattering

On green fronds and silvering,
With a light as from heaven,
The pine's dark boughs.

PABLO NERUDA COMES FLYING

For a celebration in Houston of Neruda's Centennial

With a green, articulate wave carved at the zenith
    of its potency, hungry for the pebbles of La Isla Negra,
With an inner guitar strumming a ballad of absence and
    seashells,
With chains and carnations and tangled lianas of the South
    You come flying.

With the snouts of alligators pushing through storm-drenched
    reeds,
With the aloof guanaco marching his solitary heights,
With the blazing puma and the undulant jaguar,
With the placid llama of scrupulous eye
And the secret, coiled, priestly anaconda
    You come flying.

With the granite hitching-post of the sun,
    The *Inti-Huatana* of Macchu Picchu,
With the corn men and serpents of Chichen-Itza,
With the delicate coca leaves of Mamapacha
and the plumes, brilliant, of Quetzalquatl
    You come flying.

With Andalusian oranges and Madrileño street corners,
With Castilian mesas dry and taut as drumskins,
With exit visas from the Apocalypse and a ship
    full of refugees
With the angels of Rafael Alberti and tungsten tears of Vallejo,
With Picasso's almond eyes,
With the last gaze of Miguel Hernandez
    You come flying.

With the arks of blue waters, the Antarctic leviathans,
    plunging to their hidden sanctuaries,
With the snail and the polyp and the sideways crab,
With the albatross and the anchovy,
    the penguin and the pompano
Skipping over the Humboldt Current of the Pacific
    You come flying.

With the fire of the salamander in your eyes,
With the clangorous boom of ocean in your thorax,
With a sprig of fresh laurel on your lips
And the dolorous keenings of mankind in your ears,
With strong white teeth to rip the masks off the world
    You come flying,

Oceanic, solitary, questioning,
Praising and condemning, curious and cursing,
Breaking constellations of ice,
Scribbling leaflets of quartz and *obras* of iron,
    You come flying,

Pablo Neruda
El Poeta Chileno

One hundred years
Cien anos

And there is no end
To your flight

Still, Pablo,
You come flying,

Viene volando.

AT A VATICAN EXHIBITION

Sotto voce

The slippers
Of Christ's vicar
Have crimson calfskin uppers,
Thin soles of supplest Milano leather,
Laces like white gift-wrapping ribbons
Terminating in silver-tinseled fringes
And, overall, gold brocade
Against incarnadine hide goes hitching
Heel to toe in flowing, serpentine stitching.
These, then, are the vacant slippers
Of one of the Son of Man's
Apostolic vicars.
                      Beyond, aglow
With an inward flame, notice
A triple-tiered, bejeweled tiara
Once worn on his sainted head
By the ninth Papa Pio . . .

THE UNICORN

It is the chalice of all essence
Because it does not exist. Because it cannot be,
It owns the purest of being.

We stumblers
Between moonlight and shadows
Are offering to it the merest contingency

That it might exist,
The rough salt we proffer, with which
We tease it, withhold, and, unable thus

To coax it forth
From its dark nook in the green forest,
Feed unto our too-contingent selves.

Ah, lord of the rare beasts, of the pounded salt,
That we might, improbably,
Be

And that where a dry twitching stirs
Among dry, self-writhing leaves
Might that uncombed mane,

Those prancing hooves, the magic
And sportive
Great horn,

Present themselves:
Our stamping, swift,
Companionable steed . . .

After Rilke

FOR THE SPOKEN WORD

The motions of winds inhere in our words,
But, setting down their burdens of sense,
They wheel and fly from us like lofting birds,

Leaving, as spirit leaves flesh, the uninterred
Residue of a rushing turbulence.
Recall: the motions of winds stirred within our words

Like lovers who woke with us, then quietly abjured
The offices of the day. Without pause or pretense,
They wheeled and flew from us like skittish birds,

And left, on tangled sheets, scores for unheard
Music, and ghosts of a fled eloquence.
Still, their traces, late or soon, well up within words

And living powers are with them conferred
If we but speak them aloud, by a correspondence.
So may we rise, lifting with our words

And a gift on the wing be procured
Of sounding speech in its utterance:
The riding of these motions of winds within words,
Even as we wheel them from us like lofting birds.

> *For Tommy Gay*

UNCLE KENNY

Ghostly and unknown by me,
Mangled by forceps
In difficult birthing,
We send him cards, tobacco

And, for his bad birth,
Forget him as well as can be
And do not unearth
The ghost of hard birth,

The ghastly smirk of it,
The unnerving smirk (this
Is a sane family), the forced
Forceps pinched smirk,

The —0, don't
Get hurt
In the shiny chute
Tumbling out of eternity.

You'll get strange cards
And tobacco
From your
Ghost family.

ISTHMUS

We're sitting by the ancient stone hut
Overlooking the ruins of the hidden city
Of Macchu Picchu: Javier,
East L.A. *chicano*, and me, *un guero, un gringo,*
Both of us chewing the leaf and *llibta*
And feeling the hallucinogenic buzz
From the *Cacto San Pedro*
We copped in Aguas Calientes,
Watching the clouds dance over the far forests
From this eyebrow of the jungle, this
Escarpment, an arched stone brow
Overlooking the Amazonian *selva*
And Javier tells me his American dream:
Riding on the back of a California condor
Out of the streets of the L.A. *barrio,*
Over the saw-toothed *sierras,*
The high *lagos* of Mexico,
And the green isthmus of Panama,
South to the snowy Andes
Where the bird alights and sets him down
Beside white waters of the rushing Urubamba
Then takes flight alone, and here he is,
The dream realized above these swirling clouds
In a city of stone and ghosts
Below a condor-haunted sky
And I tell him, after awhile, my American dream:
Standing on Vulcan Irazu
In the middle of the Costa Rican isthmus
So high, so cold at that elevation
Yet hot lava boiling in the caldera beneath
And in the distance the cool,
Blue line of the Pacific Ocean

And in the other direction the thin line of the Atlantic
And recalling there the wandering Arab of Al-Andaluz,
Ibn Al-Arabi, that Platonic soul
Who said this life is a brief isthmus
Between two seas, the sea of material things
And the sea of intellectual things,
Or a bridge between two such continents,
A neck, separating and uniting
The fiery and holy cauldron of the mind
And the passionate guts below,
Body and soul,
But said nothing to Javier about a soaring condor
I saw drifting overhead calling me past Irazu
Further southward toward El Peru
And wonder now was that Javier's voice there
That went calling, *"Venga, venga mas lejos conmigo."*
As his voice now says, *"Hay! Que milagros!"*
And his words float out over the gray stones
Of this ghostly sky city, drift and float now
On thermals toward Brazil, Spain, Arabia and
The unknowable seas which surround us
Where we tread North or South this brief isthmus.

MY FATHER'S WILL

When he knew he was about to die, my father
Gathered his three sons and his brother
Around our oval, oaken table.
He handed his written will to me. Read it,
He indicated, and I began reading the thing
Aloud, groping with the first sentences.

He would have read the will himself, but the thing
That was killing him was throat cancer: it
Had seized that voice my brothers
Remembered as both bell and thunder. Charged sentences
He spoke in wrath could split a table.
We'd heard his voice as Zeus, Jehovah, God the Father.

I didn't want to read the thing
But, obedient, started in on it.
After five or six sentences
He cut me off, slamming the table.
I looked up and my father
Indicated angrily that it be passed to my eldest brother.

I supposed I had done a bad job of it
And pushed the papers across to my brother.
He got only about three sentences
Into the document when my father
Pounded his fist on the oaken table
Again, shaking the thing.

Regathering his composure, my father
Directed the will be given to his brother
And once more across the table
Went the troublesome thing.
My uncle spoke firmly from the first sentence
And was allowed to read uninterrupted to the end of it.

Now, what was in it,
I don't think I remember a sentence
Of the damn thing,
Nor do my brothers.
I only recall the pounding of the table
And the rage whelming within my father.

Sitting at the same table, recalling that day, my brothers
And I speak of it in falsely casual sentences.
My father's will is still a terrible thing.

NOTES ON A MEETING

All afternoon I'm in a meeting.
Someone has left the door ajar.
Through this gap there reaches me
The stepped, several levels of a mockingbird's song
And then their sweet resolution
On a bare plane of silence, then silence's innuendo.

Come now the human words again, droning voices
Bereft of passion, enumerating
Certain discontentments, rough notes
On the problem of being human:

Notes to be duly transcribed, and the papers
Placed then in smooth, manila folders
And filed away for future reference
As if they might someday be needed

Yet no one transcribes the spiral arc
Of the mockingbird's perfect trill,
Nor the implications of its achieved completion,
Nor the sequent silence's cool innuendo.

ON MY LAST DAY

I will be reading one of the Polish poets
Talking about bread, something
Ordinary, a brown sparrow, perhaps,
Or a December sunset snagged
In bare, black branches.

The poem will remain with me all day
Like a paper cut on my finger, or
A mottled stone in my pocket, will stay
Until the kindled mirrors, with

A single breath, are extinguished
And the staring clocks, resigning
Themselves to themselves,
Must tell to the walls their solitary hours.

O water-spotted walls!
O sovereign, quickly deserted clocks!

AFTER JUSTICE

> " . . . the ancient virtue, as well as the personal signature."
>
> - Anthony Hecht

1.

After Justice was done, Justice was demanded.
The appellate courts were inundated.
While petitioners came and went, exchanging papers,
Clerks looked absently out of windows at passing birds,
Working out in their heads the math of their pensions,
Of their children's pensions.

2.

After the verdict was carefully reread
The hanged man was returned to the high gallows;
The rope was unfastened from his neck
And he was allowed to go home with
His wife, his old mother, and the two children.
"What was that all about?" asked Prose, lamely.
"Oh, drama, my boy, much mystery and drama," said Poetry,
"And they'll do it all again tomorrow."

3.

Assisted by the judiciary and the police,
The bourgeois ladies escape the proletariat.
A parakeet guards the door.

A small plaster god (or is it Chopin?)
Frowns at the street with the frown of the minor keys
But turns to the women another side: arpeggios,
Crescendos, a dying fall on a cross

And then, after much trouble
(Hell-harrowing),
The pleasing return of C major.

4.

Prospero, evening, years after the great tempest:
The shuttered pink casino goes gilt in the sunset
And the little tourist steamer, riding gaily
Above the drowned books, lurches late into the harbor.

The magician, summoning the old abracadabras,
Slips once more his black cloak off its hanger
And wistfully irons the wrinkled constellations, sighing,
Then smiling, as the mute barometer plunges.

5.

Having pursued equable treatment at the hearing,
The meters went home
Kicking cans down the street.

6.

The moon tires of being the moon and becomes
A woman in shape of a guitar, a woman
Strumming goodbye at a bus stop, goodbye to the moon,
And for miles the moon follows,
Peeping over trees and domed silos
Out there in nowhere land,
Searching madly for its truant self
As the round tires go infinitely humming.

7.

At the Mexico City Olympics, Ode Competition:
"The judge, *el juez, el es muy loco, pero corruptible,*"
Smiled my Nuevo Laredo *abogado*.
"Later, out of your prize, I must subtract
My fees, bribes, so many *morditas*."

What honor you may retrieve,
Return to the honeybees.

8.

Afterwards, a curious case of incarceration:
The poem, going nowhere, can hardly
Greet itself on the way back. The poem
That cannot hear itself has nothing to say
And has gone to sleep on the blank page.

"Sweet dreams and goodnight," a lady said,
And comforted its very tired head.

9.

After Justice declared
And was done: lingering gestures
Of retrieval, wedded to phases of the daylight,
The long-subsiding light of days swimming now
In the outer circuits of the Platonic year; then
Something like a translation, versions of Justice,
Poachings, imitations; then, nothing: a blankness,
A pause, like the spaces between stars
Hovering over a second story window
Where a light bulb shines.

10.

It is cold in America.
The Pawnee have gone under the Great Plains.
The thingness of things wants a divorce,

But from what?
Even ideas seem bits of nostalgia,
Ghosts of a dream of actuated energies.

It is very odd and cold now.
Our old futures don't call anymore

And gradations of light, moving toward a muteness, a silence,
Bend around spherical surfaces, helplessly.

"Tell me," asks the fevered, inconstant moon,
"What is the word for *good-bye*?"

11.

Donald Justice is gone. The years, his years,
The years he doesn't use anymore,
Stand like abandoned boxcars on their sidings,
Or like the black oxen in the wan fields beside them.

12. Draws Near Then The Ghost Of Chekhov As Sonya,
    Consoling

One day, uncle, the sickness
Shall pass away from the earth for good.
Some valve in the pit of the stomach
Is already closing against it. Later,
We will build a clean fire to warm our hands.
Someone climbing up from under a bridge
Will pull out a harmonica and, weakly at first,
Begin to play.
                He will find for us a tune
Recalling all that we have suffered
Through having existed, but altered,
As music alters everything.
Our work will be seen then
As clean and fine and good
And what we have suffered, all that, dear Uncle,
Will be forgotten as though it had never existed,
Only a sort of peg on which
A mouth harp player might hang loosely
The liquid drapery of a blues in G,
Revealing the beauty of our sadness
And leaving us, as beautiful things do, strangely happy.
We'll see the universe then, in the light of God's mercy,
As a field of diamonds: playful, winking diamonds.
This sadness now we'll see as sweet then,
And we'll smile. Our lives will become peaceful,
Like a caress. And we'll rest.
Dear uncle, we will rest.

13. *L'envoi*: The Absent Elegy

> *But ceasse worthy shepheard, nowe ceasse we to weery the hearers*
> *With monefull melodies, for enough our greefes be revealed...*
> — Sir Phillip Sidney

Close softly the doors.
He will not be coming back to these rooms.

The words for the elegy,
So long dwelling apart,
From other rooms are stirring
To come together now.

They were waiting, perhaps, for the rustle
Of palm fronds at Cedar Key,
The flap of a crow's wings low
Over the stubble of an Iowa field,
The sun grandly failing Miami
And Orion ascending in its place.

Now the pines for the box
Are tall enough, tall as Georgia,
And the saws whine through them.
The needle, accomplishing its work,
Comes quietly out of the sewn cloth
And is set beside its thin sisters.
The carved stone, unfelt,
Is perfectly weightless:
Its weight now is as nothing.

But the words, I'm afraid, the elegiac ones
We thought so diligent, custodial,
And passionately, to him, loyal,

The very ones he once employed:
I fear the words,
Peering out from their rooms, have halted
And are too sad now to come forth.

They are very sad, the words,
And have closed softly their doors.

For Jean Ross Justice

THE NEW POEMS

> *"I like to think that all true poems exist before their authors write them down."*
> - Donald Justice, in an interview

The new poems are lying up there, perfect
In their heaven, reclining
Like sybaritic nymphs, so comely,
Crossing the golden thighs of their texts.

How one wants to hold them!

Friend, while we are here below,
Turning up our collars to the wind,
Let me bum a cigarette. Let us smoke
And think how we might excite their pity

Or, better, their desires,
They who must yearn, passionately,
Now and then,
To play on the pulses of men.

Yes, the longer I reflect,
The more I have no doubt of it.
We must make ourselves presentable.

Tuck in your shirttail, pal,
Wipe your sleeve across your nose
And try, please, not to look like a broke monkey,

For here they come.

SOME NOTES ON THE POEMS

"The Catastrophe" owes a debt to Donald Justice's poem, "The Assassination." "Sea Wind, Pompano" owes a debt to both Rilke's "Lied vom Meer (Capri, Piccola Marina)" and Justice's "Sea Wind: A Song." "Codicil To Be Appended To The City Charter" rehearses some of Euripedes' "The Bacchantes." "The Dead" owes a debt to an eponymous poem by Angel Gonzalez. "Others: To Adam Zagajewski" references Zagajewski's "To Go To Lvov" and also owes something to conversation with the poet about Lvov. "Tycho Brahe's *Nova Stella*" was inspired in part by an essay on Poe by Richard Wilbur. "Life 101" steals a phrase from Hart Crane, for which theft my unconscious is responsible. "Requital For Fire" employs imagery gleaned from Heraclitus' fragments. The Tolstoy poem is adapted from various translations of *War and Peace*. "Wild Turkeys At Paisano" borrows a simile from the work of Justice. "Pablo Neruda Comes Flying" borrows its central trope from an early poem by Neruda and not, as some mistake, from Elizabeth Bishop, who, I think, herself borrowed from the same Neruda poem. "The Unicorn" is indebted to an eponymous poem by Rilke. "After Justice" freely echoes the work of Donald Justice, my teacher, friend and mentor. In the epigraph to "The New Poems" the interviewer was the poet Dana Gioia.

BIOGRAPHICAL NOTE

Daniel Christopher Rifenburgh was born May 24, 1949 in Elmira, New York. He attended the University of Louisville and served three years in the U.S. Army during the Vietnam War, working as a military journalist. He completed a BA at Florida Atlantic University in 1981 and earned an MA from the University of Florida in 1987. He received the Robert H. Winner Memorial Award from the Poetry Society of America in 1996. His first book, *Advent*, was published in London by Waywiser Press in 2002 and received the Natalie Ornish Award from the Texas Institute of Letters (TIL). He was awarded a Dobie Paisano Fellowship from the University of Texas and the TIL in 2005. He was also invited to serve as a workshop instructor and editor on the National Endowment For the Arts *Operation Homecoming* initiative and the resulting anthology. His work has appeared in *Paris Review, The New Republic, Southwest Review, New Criterion* and other distinguished journals. After some years of college adjunct teaching he now drives an 18-wheeler flatbed rig, hauling steel out of the Port of Houston.

Mutabilis Press is a non-profit literary press dedicated to the publication of poetry, with focus on writers living or working in Houston and the surrounding area

♦ ♦ ♦

For more information, see www.mutabilispress.org